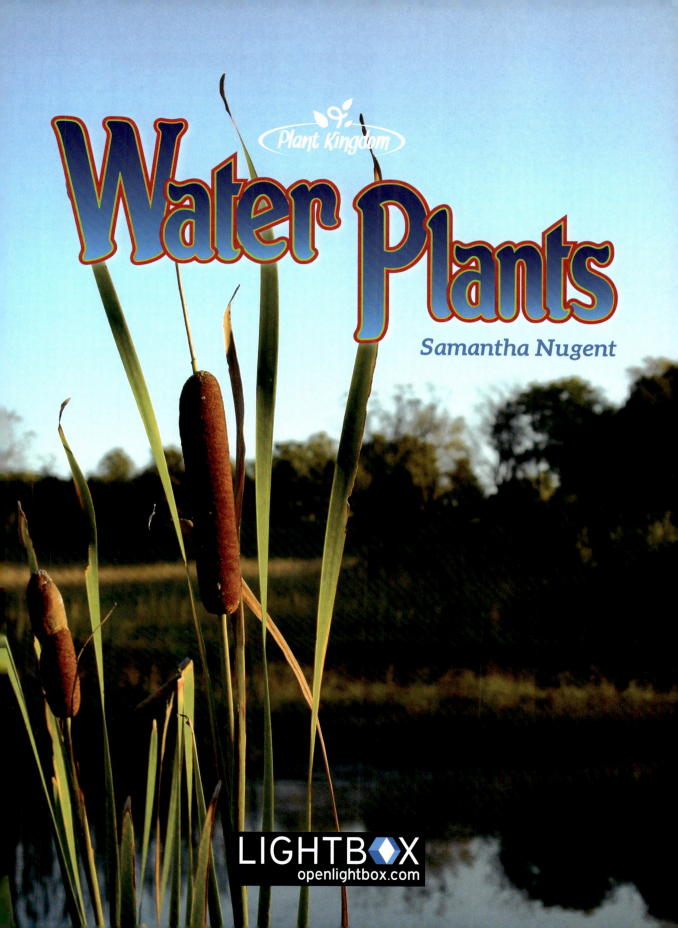

Plant Kingdom

# Water Plants

Samantha Nugent

LIGHTBOX
openlightbox.com

# LIGHTBOX

Go to
**www.openlightbox.com**
and enter this book's
unique code.

**ACCESS CODE**

## LBU38837

Lightbox is an all-inclusive digital solution for the teaching and learning of curriculum topics in an original, groundbreaking way. Lightbox is based on National Curriculum Standards.

# STANDARD FEATURES OF LIGHTBOX

**AUDIO** High-quality narration using text-to-speech system

**VIDEOS** Embedded high-definition video clips

**ACTIVITIES** Printable PDFs that can be emailed and graded

**WEBLINKS** Curated links to external, child-safe resources

**SLIDESHOWS** Pictorial overviews of key concepts

**TRANSPARENCIES** Step-by-step layering of maps, diagrams, charts, and timelines

**INTERACTIVE MAPS** Interactive maps and aerial satellite imagery

**QUIZZES** Ten multiple choice questions that are automatically graded and emailed for teacher assessment

**KEY WORDS** Matching key concepts to their definitions

# CONTENTS

# Introducing Plants

Plants can be found all over the world. They can survive everywhere from the ocean floor to parched deserts. Plants come in many shapes and sizes, but they all have common needs.

All plants need sunshine, water, and air to survive. Plants use these things to make their own food through a process called **photosynthesis**. Most plants also need soil to grow **roots**.

Some floating plants are not anchored to the ground by roots.

# Built for the Water

There are many plant **species** on Earth. Plants have adapted, or changed slowly over time, to suit their **environments**. Some plants have even adapted to live in the water.

Plants are categorized by their features. Water plants fit into three groups. Emergent plants grow partially underwater, submergent plants grow totally underwater, and floating plants float on top of the water.

The ancestors **of all plants** grew in the water.

**Seagrasses are the only plants that grow flowers underwater.**

Some types of **water lily can grow** to be more than **8 feet wide.** (2.4 meters)

## Photosynthesis

Plants use a process called photosynthesis to make food. The green pigments in leaves, called **chlorophyll**, capture energy from the Sun. The leaves also take in carbon dioxide through openings called stomata. The plant's roots absorb water, which is transported into the leaves. The energy from the Sun turns water and carbon dioxide into oxygen, and a sugar called glucose. The plant uses glucose as food for energy. Then, the leaves release oxygen back into the air.

sunlight

oxygen
leaves
chlorophyll
stomata
carbon dioxide
stem
roots
water

# Water Plants

## A life in water presents unique challenges for plants.

The Sun's rays must travel through water before they reach the submergent plants that grow beneath the surface. Water weakens the Sun's rays. This makes photosynthesis more challenging. Although some water plants have adapted to low levels of sunlight, they cannot grow in very deep water where there is no sunlight at all.

Plants that grow underwater must also pull carbon dioxide from the water instead of the air. To overcome this obstacle, some submergent plants can use a chemical called bicarbonate during photosynthesis. There is often more bicarbonate present in water than there is carbon dioxide.

Large water plants, such as mangrove trees, have wide root systems to prevent them from tipping over. Wide roots keep mangrove trees firmly anchored in soft soil and protect them against rough ocean waters. Many aquatic trees have roots that stick out of the water. They use these roots to take in the oxygen they need for photosynthesis.

Bald cypresses grow very slowly, but they are capable of living very long lives.

# Functions of Water Lily Parts

## Flowers
Plants grow flowers in order to reproduce. Flowers produce seeds from which new plants can grow. A flower is able to make seeds when it has been **pollinated**. Animals such as bees and butterflies help spread pollen. Water plants, such as water lilies, grow their flowers outside of the water.

## Leaves
Plant leaves are protected by a waxy coating called a cuticle. It protects delicate plant structures from harmful chemicals. The cuticle also helps keep water from evaporating out of the plant. Unlike plants that grow on land, water plants do not dry out easily.

## Stems
Plant stems house the thin tubes that carry water and **nutrients** from the roots to the leaves. Green stems also contain chlorophyll. This means they can perform photosynthesis. Plants that float on water have soft stems. Aquatic trees and plants that grow in moving water need firm stems for more support.

## Roots
Roots take in water and nutrients, and prevent plants from toppling over. The roots of floating plants are always exposed to water and nutrients. They do not need to waste energy growing large roots.

# How Do Water Plants Grow?

**Humans and animals have senses that tell them about their surroundings.** Senses are used to find food, escape danger, and find mates. Plants also respond to forces in their environment, known as stimuli.

Plant senses are called tropisms. They make it possible for plants to move toward sunlight and grow roots toward water. Tropisms also help plants stay upright. Responding to stimuli helps plants to survive better in their environments.

Light enters water to depths of approximately 3,280 feet (1,000 m), but it becomes weaker the deeper it travels.

Plants detect and respond to sunlight through a tropism called phototropism. Some wavelengths of light cannot move freely through water. In response to this, submergent plants are especially sensitive to blue light, a frequency that does travel freely through water.

Plants sense and respond to chemicals in their environment. This is called chemotropism. Water plants are sensitive to changes in acid and salt. When a water plant feels stressed, it makes a chemical called abscisic acid (ABA). ABA causes responses to protect the plant from harm. These include closing its stomata, growing leaves that sit at the surface of the water, and preventing seeds from sprouting.

In cold **climates**, ice often forms on top of water and blocks the Sun's rays. Although some water plants can survive cold water temperatures below the ice, many stop growing during this time. Other submergent plants continue photosynthesizing with the limited light that reaches them. When the ice melts in spring, water plants grow again.

**Some submergent plants only come to the surface to produce flowers.**

**Red leaves** help some water plants take in more **blue light.**

**Bladderwort plants are sensitive to touch.**

# From Seed to Plant

**Many water plants begin life as a seed. These seeds are spread with the help of wind, water, and animals.**

### Seed

Seeds develop inside the flowers of water plants. Seeds start to form once a flower has been pollinated with the pollen of another plant from the same species. Sometimes, a flower will be pollinated with its own pollen.

A plant is ready to produce seeds when cells within the pollen attach to a part of the flower called the pistil. Depending on their species, water plants develop flowers in the spring and summer months. By autumn, the seeds are ready to spread to a new location and begin growing.

## Sprout

Seeds need water, soil, and mild temperatures to sprout. If the conditions are not right, the seeds may not sprout. Animals help seeds with a protective shell prepare to sprout. When animals eat, digest, and pass these seeds through their bodies, the seeds lose their protective shells. The first parts of the plant to grow are the roots. Shortly after, the plant's stem and leaves start to grow.

## Mature Plant

After sprouting, young plants grow toward sunlight. As they grow, the thin, white sprouts develop color. Water plants reach adulthood, or mature, when they can grow flowers. The mature plant's flowers can then be pollinated, so they can develop their own seeds.

# Exploring Habitats

**Water plants have adapted to survive in a wide variety of different homes, or habitats.** They can survive in both salt and fresh water environments, as well as still and moving waters. Each habitat presents unique challenges that water plants must overcome.

## Salt Water

Salt water is found in the ocean, as well as in some **wetlands**. Some saltwater environments, such as estuaries, have varied salt content. Estuaries are places where freshwater rivers meet the ocean. Salt water from the ocean flows into the river and makes the water salty. Water plants in these habitats must adapt quickly to these changes. Some plants, such as cordgrass, can get rid of extra salt through their leaves. This stops them from drying out.

## Fresh Water

Earth's streams, rivers, and lakes are home to many freshwater plants. Still wetlands have very little oxygen and few minerals. Dead plants do not break down easily in low-oxygen waters. These waters become very acidic as a result. Many water plants cannot survive these conditions. Those that do survive have specialized parts to help them gain nutrients and oxygen in their environment. Some wetland plants have adapted to gain nutrients from the bodies of animals.

## Case Study: Bald Cypresses

Bald cypress trees are sometimes called swamp cypresses. They grow in the slow-moving waters of swamps in the southern part of North America. Bald cypresses can grow to be more than 100 feet tall (30.5 m).

The bases of bald cypress trunks have been known to grow more than 3 feet (1 m) thick. In addition to its thick trunk and deep roots, the bald cypress also grows woody "knees" beside its trunk. Scientists believe these knees help the trees stay upright in soft soil.

Bald cypresses are one of the few coniferous trees that lose their leaves. They do this when they feel stressed by changes in their environment. Without leaves, the bald cypress can save energy by stopping its own growth until its environment improves.

**Tidal marshes** are only filled with **water for part** of **each day**.

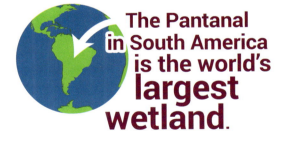

**The Pantanal in South America is the world's largest wetland**.

Some **freshwater plants send pollen into the air with explosive bursts**.

Water plants rely on the animals that live in their ecosystem. Ducks and other birds help to spread water plant seeds to new locations.

# Water Ecosystems

**All living beings on Earth rely on their environment for survival.** Plants and animals also rely on each other for food, shelter, and other needs. These relationships are known as **ecosystems**. Water plants play an important role in many ecosystems.

Water ecosystems are home to a variety of birds, reptiles, insects, and other animals. Some animals, such as fish and clams, spend their entire lives in the water. Others rely on the plants and animals that live in the water for food. The roots of mangrove trees provide a safe place for young reef fish to hide from predators. Manatees feed on seagrass that grows in shallow waters.

Water plants play a role in the conditions of their environment. Reeds and rushes help prevent rivers and streams from eroding. Water plants can also help produce the oxygen that fish and other aquatic animals need to survive. When they die, water plants break down and add nutrients to the soil, helping new plants grow.

# Food Chain

A **food chain** shows the order in which energy moves through **organisms**. This is a part of how an ecosystem works. Water plants are part of the food chains in their environment. They act as **producers**.

**Consumers** can be primary, secondary, or tertiary. A primary consumer eats plants. A secondary consumer eats primary consumers. A tertiary consumer eats secondary consumers.

**4** ## Tertiary Consumer—River Otter
River otters are consumers. They eat meat to gain energy. They are called apex predators because no other animals hunt them.

**3** ## Secondary Consumer—Crayfish
Crayfish are consumers. They are omnivores, which means they eat both plants and animals. Crayfish are hunted by larger meat-eating animals, known as carnivores.

**2** ## Primary Consumer—Snail
Snails are consumers. This means they must eat other living things. Snails are herbivores, or plant-eating animals.

**1** ## Producer—Pondweed
Pondweed is a producer. This means it makes its own food through photosynthesis.

# Water Plants Around the World

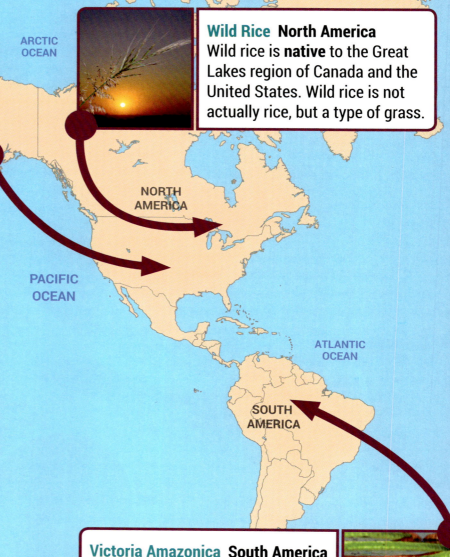

**ARCTIC OCEAN**

## Wild Rice  North America
Wild rice is **native** to the Great Lakes region of Canada and the United States. Wild rice is not actually rice, but a type of grass.

## Bladderwort
**North America**
Bladderworts are carnivorous water plants. They trap insects to eat using small containers, called bladders, on their leaves. Bladderworts grow in lakes and streams all over the world. The common species is native to North America.

**NORTH AMERICA**

**PACIFIC OCEAN**

**ATLANTIC OCEAN**

**SOUTH AMERICA**

N

| 0 | 621 Miles |
|---|---|
| 0 | 1000 Kilometers |

### MAP LEGEND
☐ Land
☐ Water

## Victoria Amazonica  South America
Victoria amazonica is also known as the giant water lily. This floating water plant is found in the Amazon Basin of South America.

**Water plants are found almost everywhere on Earth.** They adapt to changes in their environment. Over time, some plants change enough that they become a new species. Water plants often change when they spread to new places. People help spread water plants by catching them in fishing equipment, boats, or clothing.

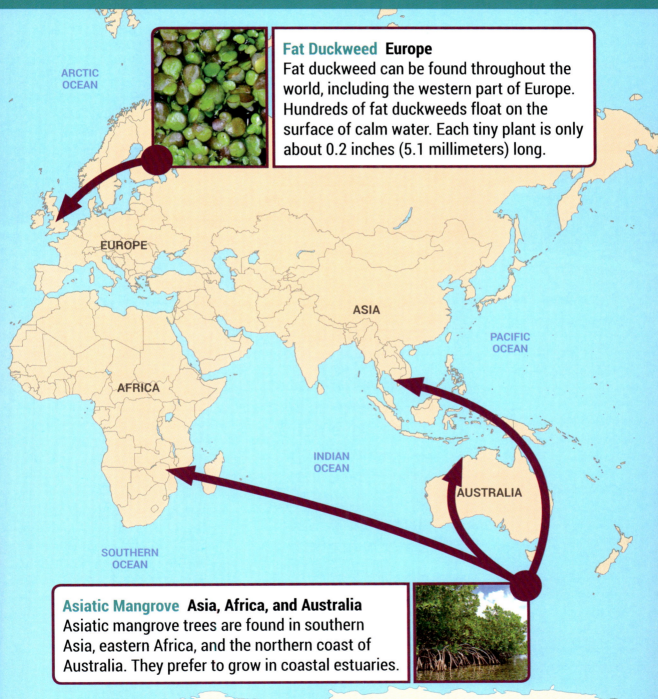

**Fat Duckweed  Europe**
Fat duckweed can be found throughout the world, including the western part of Europe. Hundreds of fat duckweeds float on the surface of calm water. Each tiny plant is only about 0.2 inches (5.1 millimeters) long.

**Asiatic Mangrove  Asia, Africa, and Australia**
Asiatic mangrove trees are found in southern Asia, eastern Africa, and the northern coast of Australia. They prefer to grow in coastal estuaries.

# Issues Facing Water Plants

People pull water from lakes and ponds to water crops. They also build dams to block the flow of rivers. This can upset the natural environment and make it hard for some water plants to survive.

Pollution can also threaten water plants and their ecosystems. Chemicals from industrial activities can kill water plants. Some water plants take in pollution from their environments. These harmful chemicals are then passed on to animals that eat them.

### 1849 to 1860

Three Swamp Lands Acts are passed in the United States. It becomes legal to drain wetlands in order to build human settlements.

### 1948

The Federal Water Pollution Control Act is put into place. Also known as the Clean Water Act, this act is the first of its kind in the United States. It puts laws in place to protect water habitats from pollution.

### 1960s

Hydrilla grows out of control in American freshwater ecosystems. The plant was brought to the United States in the early 1950s for use in aquariums. It is still a problem in many lakes and rivers today.

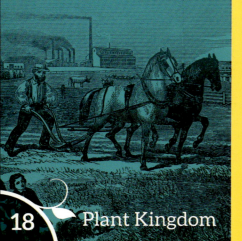

Wetlands are often drained so that the land can be used for farming. In nature, wetlands act as a sponge. They take in excess water from rainfall and melting snow. When wetlands are emptied, extra water has no place to drain. This causes flooding that can damage crops and the natural environment.

In nature, ecosystems are balanced. When one group of animals becomes too large, it can be hard for others to survive. Too much waste in water ecosystems makes water plant populations grow larger than they naturally would. More plants make it easier for animals to hide, which makes hunting harder for the animals that rely on them for food. Too many floating water plants can block sunlight and prevent submergent plants from growing.

## 1973
The **Endangered** Species Act is passed in the United States. It becomes illegal to remove or otherwise damage endangered plants in their natural habitat.

## 2001
The month of March is officially named Seagrass Awareness Month in Florida. People can learn about the importance of seagrass at events held across the state each year.

## 2011
A dam is removed from the Elwha River, allowing water plants to return to the river. This is the largest dam removal in United States history.

# Activity

## Water Plant Life Cycle

Choose a species of water plant that interests you. Research in the library or online to find out more about the life cycle of your chosen water plant. Make notes about each stage. How is the life cycle of your plant similar to or different from the life cycles of other water plants? Do you notice any similarities to or differences from the life cycles of plants that live on dry land?

## Materials

- a large sheet of paper

- colored pencils or markers

- books about plants or access to the internet

## Steps

1. Draw three big circles on your sheet of paper. Label them seed, sprout, and mature plant.

2. Draw arrows between the circles to show the correct sequence of the life cycle.

3. List the facts you discover inside the circles for each stage of the life cycle.

# Water Plant Quiz

1. What are the three groups of water plants?

2. What is one way that reeds and rushes help river environments?

3. When was the Endangered Species Act passed in the United States?

4. Which month was named Seagrass Awareness Month in Florida?

5. How do wetlands prevent flooding?

6. What is the name for plant senses?

7. On what continent do Victoria amazonica plants grow?

8. What part of a plant is responsible for making seeds?

9. What are consumers?

10. Why are some plants' stems green?

**ANSWERS:**

1. Emergent, submergent, and floating   2. They prevent erosion
3. 1973   4. March   5. They hold excess water from rain and melted snow   6. Tropisms
7. South America   8. The flowers   9. Animals or plants that eat other animals or plants
10. They contain chlorophyll

# Key Words

**chlorophyll:** a pigment, or color, in leaves that makes them appear green

**climates:** the average weather conditions of regions over a period of time

**consumers:** animals or plants that eat other animals or plants

**ecosystems:** environments where many animals and plants live together and depend upon each other for survival

**endangered:** a plant or animal that is threatened with becoming extinct

**environments:** the living and non-living things in areas that affect organisms living there

**food chain:** the order that energy moves through organisms; the system in which organisms rely on each other for food

**native:** belonging to a particular place

**nutrients:** substances that organisms need in order to live

**organisms:** living things made up of one or more cells

**photosynthesis:** the way plants change carbon dioxide and water into food and oxygen

**pollinated:** spread pollen grains to flowers so fruit can form

**producers:** organisms that make their own food

**roots:** parts used to attach plants to the ground

**species:** a related group of animals or plants

**wetlands:** areas of Earth where the ground is wet for at least some of the year

# Index

# LIGHTB⬦X

## ➕ SUPPLEMENTARY RESOURCES

Click on the plus icon ➕ found in the bottom left corner of each spread to open additional teacher resources.

- Download and print the book's quizzes and activities
- Access curriculum correlations
- Explore additional web applications that enhance the Lightbox experience

## LIGHTBOX DIGITAL TITLES
### Packed full of integrated media

**VIDEOS**

**INTERACTIVE MAPS**

**WEBLINKS**

**SLIDESHOWS**

**QUIZZES**

### OPTIMIZED FOR

- ✓ TABLETS
- ✓ WHITEBOARDS
- ✓ COMPUTERS
- ✓ AND MUCH MORE!

Published by Smartbook Media Inc.
350 5th Avenue, 59th Floor
New York, NY 10118
Website: www.openlightbox.com

Library of Congress Cataloging-in-Publication Data

Names: Nugent, Samantha.
Title: Water plants / Samantha Nugent.
Description: New York, NY : Smartbook Media, Inc., [2017] | Series: Plant kingdom | Includes index.
Identifiers: LCCN 2016020126 (print) | LCCN 2016021645 (ebook) | ISBN 9781510514133 (hard cover : alk. paper) | ISBN 9781510514140 (Multi-user ebk.)
Subjects: LCSH: Aquatic plants–Juvenile literature.

Classification: LCC QK916 .N84 2017 (print) | LCC QK916 (ebook) | DDC 581.7/6--dc23
LC record available at https://lccn.loc.gov/2016020126

Printed in Brainerd, Minnesota, United States
1 2 3 4 5 6 7 8 9 0  20 19 18 17 16

062016
150616

Editor: Katie Gillespie
Designer: Tom Magee

Photo Credits
Every reasonable effort has been made to trace ownership and to obtain permission to reprint copyright material. The publisher would be pleased to have any errors or omissions brought to its attention so that they may be corrected in subsequent printings. The publisher acknowledges Getty Images, iStock, and Alamy as its primary image suppliers for this title.